PERFECTION LEARNING®

Forming
Hypotheses

Cathy Elliott

Table of Contents

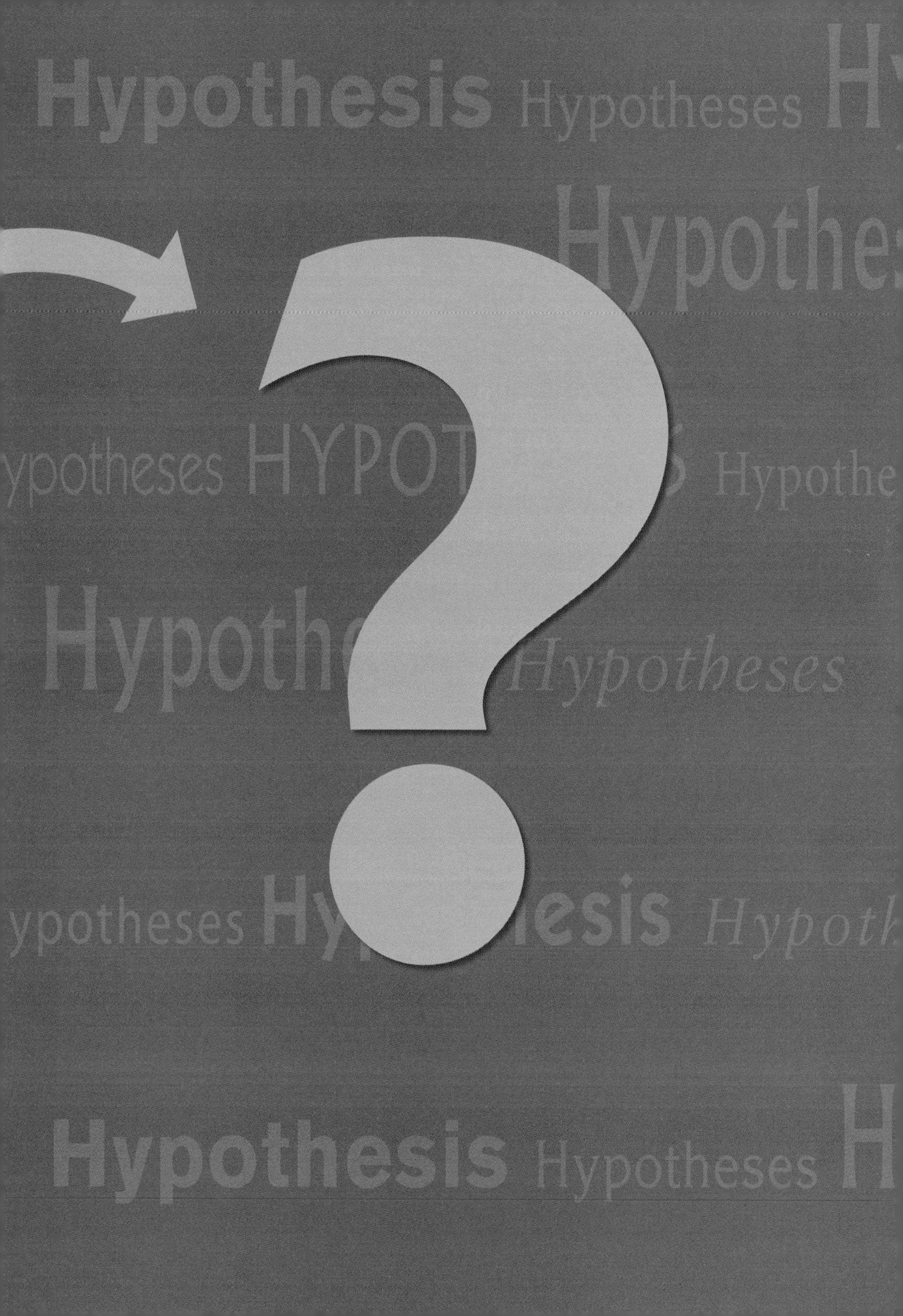

Introduction

After playing outside all morning, you wonder if lunch is ready. You run inside and see that it is almost noon. You know that your dad usually makes lunch at noon. So you guess that your lunch is probably almost ready.

This educated guess is a **hypothesis**. You started with the question, Is lunch ready? You based your hypothesis, that lunch was almost ready, on your **observation**

of the time and that your dad usually makes lunch at noon.

Scientists form hypotheses through observation, as well. Then they conduct **experiments**, record the outcomes of these experiments, and decide whether or not their hypotheses were correct.

This process of conducting experiments to test hypotheses is the **scientific method**. Let's learn more about this method.

The word *hypotheses* is plural. *Hypothesis* is the singular form.

1

The Scientific Method

Here's how the scientific method works.

Choose a problem or question.
Make observations and **investigate** your topic.
Form a hypothesis based on your observations.
Create an experiment to test the hypothesis.
Reflect on your findings and hypothesis.
Share what you found with others.

You can see that the whole experiment is based on the hypothesis. That is why it is so important to make careful observations before you form your hypothesis.

A hypothesis is just about to be tested in Mrs. Randolph's class. Let's see what happens.

2

The Snail Experiment

Mrs. Randolph's class has been observing a number of snails that live inside an aquarium in the classroom. Each day, the students stop by and see the snails. They tap on the glass and talk about what they see.

SLiMy SNaiL ASide

Snails are neither male nor female. They are both.

Almost all of the snails are hanging upside down from the glass lid. The students are no longer surprised. It happens every day, even when they place the snails on the bottom of the tank the night before. They record their findings in their notebooks.

One day, Mrs. Randolph says, "Class, you are so good at watching our snails and recording what you see. You know a lot about how snails behave."

She brings the aquarium over to the table. "Today, we are going to conduct an experiment. We will try to find the answer to this question:

Would a snail rather hang upside down or sit right side up?"

Hypothesis Hypotheses

"Upside down! Upside down!" the students yell in agreement.

"Why do you think so?" Mrs. Randolph asks as she hands out a plastic lid to each student.

"Because we have seen it," Chelsea says. "Every day."

"I wrote it in my notebook!" Lawrence says as he holds up a spiral-bound book. "It's all in here."

SLiMy SNaiL ASide

Snails' eyes are poised at the ends of two long tentacles called *stalks*.

3

What's Your Hypothesis?

Mrs. Randolph stops handing out the lids for a moment. "So what is your hypothesis?"

Together, the children decide on their hypothesis:

A snail would rather hang upside down than sit right side up.

"Let's find out if your hypothesis is correct!" Mrs. Randolph says.

SLiMy SNaiL ASide

The Roman snail can live up to 30 years.

Mrs. Randolph asks each child to take a snail and place it on a plastic lid until the snail attaches. Then the children turn the lids over. Now the snails are hanging upside down. Time to observe and see what happens.

"Ooooh. Mine is so slimy!" Jamie says. He touches the snail's shell.

Twenty minutes pass. What has happened? The class finds that every snail has climbed over the side of the lid. Now all the snails are on top of the lids.

The class tries turning over the lids again, but everyone gets the same result. It seems the snails like to sit right side up. The hypothesis is wrong!

4

A Successful Experiment

So why are the snails upside down every morning? No one seems to know.

Mrs. Randolph asks, "Could there be other reasons the snails slide up to the ceiling?"

That question starts the class thinking. Ricardo says, "Maybe they are trying to get out of the aquarium. But on the plastic lid, they are already out."

SLiMy SNaiL ASide

Snails cannot hear.

"That would be a good reason," Mrs. Randolph says. "Or maybe there is another reason. But even though our hypothesis was wrong, our experiment was still a success.

"Scientists also form hypotheses that are not always correct. More important than forming a correct hypothesis is continuing to ask questions and test things to find out more about the world."

5

More Questions About Snails

Using land snails and a few simple materials around the house or classroom, set up experiments to answer these questions and practice forming hypotheses.

SLiMy SNaiL ASide

Garden snails are nocturnal animals—active at night.

Hunker Down in That Habitat

Question: Do snails prefer rocks or leaves for their **habitat**?

Form a hypothesis: Snails prefer _____ for their habitat.

Test the hypothesis:

Materials:

2 snails, rocks, leaves

Procedure:

- Place a snail at an equal distance from a pile of rocks and a pile of leaves.

- See which pile the snail chooses.

- Record your findings.
- Repeat the experiment with another snail.

What can you conclude? Was your hypothesis correct?

At a Snail's Pace

Question: How far can a snail travel in 10 minutes?

Form a hypothesis: A snail can travel _____ in 10 minutes.

Test the hypothesis:

Materials:

snail, spray bottle of water, black paper, string, and ruler

Procedure:

- Spray the snail 5 or 6 times with a light mist of water.

- Put the snail on black paper and wait 10 minutes.

- Remove the snail from the paper.

- Measure the distance that the snail moved on the paper using string.

- Measure the string with a ruler and record your findings.

What can you conclude? Was your hypothesis correct?

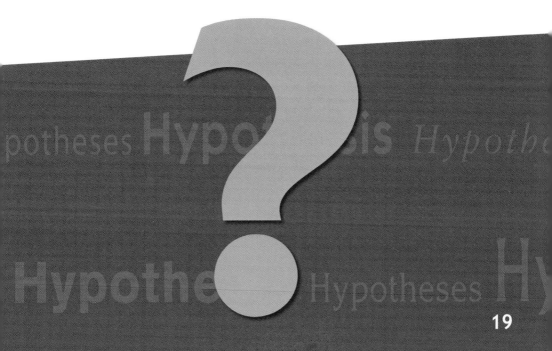

The Favorite Meal

Question: What is a snail's favorite food?

Form a hypothesis: _____ is a snail's favorite food.

Test the hypothesis:

Materials:

snail

bits of lettuce, carrot, banana, and orange

Procedure:

- Place each kind of food in the snail's habitat at equal distances from the snail.

- Observe the snail's behavior.

- After the snail begins to feed, record your findings.

What can you conclude? Was your hypothesis correct?

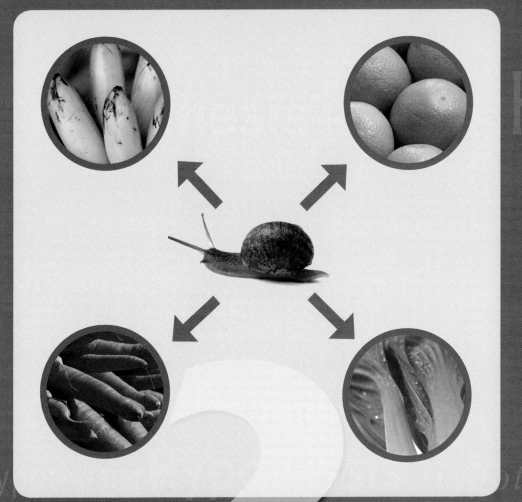

Glossary

experiment	controlled test or investigation
habitat	environment where a plant or animal naturally lives
hypothesis	educated guess
investigate	observe or study closely
observation	act of noticing or paying attention
scientific method	process scientists use to answer questions

Index

Hypothesis Hypotheses